Ab......

Edited by Tony Chatterton M.Litt

Marlinspike Press

Tinfish Type - Librarie du Levant 2019 - Marlinspike 17291

Third Edition

Marlinspike Press Inc.
Marlinspike Building, Marlinspike Place, Greenwich Conn.

Beowulf – Abridged for Schools and Colleges

This abridged version of the epic poem is based upon two authoritative translations of the Nowell Codex manuscript. Whereas the full poem is just over 3,000 lines, this abridged version runs to 1,775 lines. Digressions and genealogies (apart from Hrothgar's) have been removed, leaving a clear narrative that focuses on the character of Beowulf and the events surrounding him.

It includes a guide to the characters, the history of the poem, a brief summary, a short prose version and activities for the classroom.

Contents

Introduction

Beowulf is an epic Anglo-Saxon poem which is both subtle and savage. For many English speakers it is the first great epic, one that brings vividly to life their forefathers and their love of war, sea, and adventure.

The following abridged translation of *Beowulf* has been written for the classroom and for the would-be Anglo-Saxon scholar wanting an accessible introduction to the poem. In order to please both readers, a regular cadence has been used which permits the reader to see ahead. The measure used in the present translation is believed to be as near a reproduction of the original as modern English affords. End-rhyme has been used occasionally; internal rhyme, sporadically.

An effort has been made to give a decidedly archaic flavour to a number of lines. However, while some archaic words have been used they are unlikely to prevent the reader from understanding or enjoying the story as it unfolds.

Commentary

The opening of *Beowulf* often wrong-foots the reader with its reference to Hrothgar's grandfather, Beow(ulf). Yet this Danish Beow isn't the main character. The eponymous Beowulf is a Swedish Geat and only appears after Grendel has attacked Hrothgar's mead hall. The reader is given a brief genealogy before the action begins.

BEOWULF

I The Life and Death of Scyld, the Founder of the Danish House (The Scyldings were a famous race of Spear-Danes.)

LO, praise the glory of the people's king,
and the spear-armed Danes, in days long sped.
Scyld was their mighty king, and in his honour
His people are called Scyldings.
Those by the whale-road*, heard his demands,
gave him golden gifts: a good king he!
To him a strong heir was born, Beow,
a son in his halls, whom heaven sent
to favour the folk with a willing warrior.
Famed was this Beow, and far flew
the Dane's fame in Scandian lands.

In time Scyld left his blessed life
and sailed to the All-Father's keeping,
grieved his loving clansmen, the death of
Scyld, the leader beloved who long had ruled.
They laid their lord in an atheling's barge
filled with treasure fetched from afar.
No ship have I known so nobly weighted
with weapons of war and spoil of battle,
with breastplate and blade. On his chest lay
a heaped hoard that hence should go
far over the sea with him, floating away.
High over his head they hoist the standard,
a golden banner; let billows take him
to the ocean. Grave were their spirits,
mournful their mood.

II Scyld's Successors – Hrothgar's Great Mead Hall
(The Danish Beow succeeds his father Scyld.)

NOW Beow led the Scyldings,
leader beloved, and long he ruled
in fame with all folk, till awoke his heir,
Hrothgar. To him was given such glory of war,
such honour of combat, that all his kin
obeyed him gladly till great grew his band
of youthful warriors. It came in his mind
to bid his henchmen to build a hall,
a master mead-house, mightier far
than ever was seen by the sons of earth.
Wide, I heard, was the work commanded,
for many a tribe this middle-earth round,
laboured to build the hall. It fell, as he ordered,
in rapid achievement that ready it stood there,
of halls the noblest: Heorot he named it
whose message had might in many a land.
Not reckless of promise, rings he gave out,
treasure at the banquet: there towered the hall,
high, gabled wide with swords, antlers and hide.

But lo, with envy and anger an evil spirit
endured the day in his dark abode,
then heard each night the din of revel
high in the hall: there harps rang out,
clear song of the singer who sang
tales of the early time of man,
how the Almighty made the earth,
fairest fields enfolded by water,
set, triumphant, sun and moon
for a light to lighten the land-dwellers.
So lived the clansmen in cheer and revel
a joyful life, till the fiend began
to fashion evils, in that field of hell.

Grendel this monster grim was called,
marsh-dweller, marsh-stepper,
mighty in moorland living,
in fen and fastness; chief of the giants.
Banished by the Creator and damned by him.
Kin of Cain and cursed with Abel's slaughter.
Ill fared his fate, and far was he driven,
for the slaughter's sake, from sight of men.
Branded and banned like Cain,
waker of all that woeful breed:
demons and elves and evil-spirits
and giants that grappled with God.

III Grendel the Murderer (Grendel attacks the Danes.)

AT fall of night Grendel crept forth to find
that haughty house, and silence forever
the Ring-Danes who revelled loudly.
In Heorot he found the atheling band
asleep after feasting and fearless of sorrow,
or human hardship. Unhallowed creature,
grim and greedy, he grasped sleeping men,
wrathful, reckless, from their resting-places.
Thirty of Hrothgar's thanes he plucked
and thence he rushed homeward
full of foulest spoil, faring fenward,
laden with slaughter, his dank lair to seek.

Then at the dawning, as grey day was breaking,
the might of Grendel to men was known;
then was wail uplifted, loud moan in the morn.
Hrothgar, the mighty chief, sat dejectedly
and laboured in woe for the loss of his thanes.
A few brave Scyldings traced the trail of the fiend,
spirit accursed, but too cruel that sorrow,
too long the path, too loathsome.

And at fen's night returning,
Anew began ruthless, bloody murder,
Grendel, death's wrecker-demon,
determined in guilt and murderous malice.
They were easy to find, those who elsewhere
sought to hide remote from the rest,
in forest and byre, cowering and unblessed,
most baneful of burden the wails at night.
No matter how far or fast, the fiend outran
the child, the mother, the terrified man!
Thus Grendel ruled unrighteous and raged his fill
one against all; until empty stood
that lordly building, and long it remained so.
Twelve years' tide the trouble Hrothgar bore,
twelve winters' time torture suffered,
sovereign of Scyldings, sorrows in plenty,
boundless cares. There came unhidden
tidings true to the tribes of men,
in sorrowful songs, how ceaselessly Grendel
harassed Hrothgar, what hate he bore him,
what murder and massacre, many a year,
the evil one ambushed old and young
death-shadow dark, and dogged them still,
lured, or lurked in the livelong night
of misty moorlands and forbidden fens.

Such heaping of horrors the hater of men,
lonely roamer, wrought unceasing,
harassings heavy. Over Heorot he lorded,
gold-bright hall, in gloomy nights;
and never could Hrothgar approach his throne.
Sore was the sorrow to the Scyldings' friends,
heart-rending misery. Many nobles
sat assembled, and searched out counsel
how it were best for bold-hearted men
to try their hand against harassing terror.

IV Beowulf Goes to Hrothgar's Assistance

THIS heard in his home, Hygelac's thane,
great among Geats, of Grendel's doings.
Beowulf was the mightiest man of valour
stalwart and stately. A stout wave-walker
he bade make ready. 'King Hrothgar,' said he,
'far o'er the swan-road seeks help.'
And now the bold one from bands of Geats
with comrades chosen, the keenest of warriors
ever found; with fourteen men leaves
the land's confines; afloat was the ship,
boat under bluff. On board they climbed,
warriors ready; waves were churning
sea with sand; the sailors bore
on the breast of the bark their bright array,
their mail and weapons: the men rowed off,
on their willing way, the well-braced craft.
Then moved over the waters by might of the wind
that bark like a bird with breast of foam,
till in season due, on the second day,
the curved prow such course had run
that sailors now could see the land,
sea-cliffs shining, steep high hills,
headlands broad. Their haven was found,
their journey ended. Up then quickly
Beowulf's clansmen climbed ashore,
anchored their vessel, with armour clashing
and gear of battle: God they thanked
for passing in peace over the paths of the sea.

Now saw from the cliff a Scylding clansman,
a warden that watched the water-side,
how they bore over the gangway glittering shields,
war-gear in readiness; wonder seized him
to know what manner of men they were.

Straight to the strand his steed he rode,
Hrothgar's henchman; with hand of might
he shook his spear, and spoke in parley.
'Who are ye, then, ye armed men,
mailed folk, that in your mighty vessel
have crossed the roaring ocean's way,
and landed here? A watchman I,
sentinel set over the sea-marshes,
lest any foe to the folk of Danes
with harrying fleet should harm the land.
Yet bolder warriors from afar never I saw.
Now, dwellers, ocean-travellers, who are you
and what reason brings you here?'

To him Beowulf spoke in answer;
the warriors' leader his word-hoard unlocked:
'We are by kin of the clan of Geats,
and Hygelac's own hearth-fellows we.
To thy lord and liege in loyal mood
we hasten hither, come on errand.
We hear the sayings of ocean men,
that amid the Scyldings a scathing monster,
dark ill-doer, in dusky winter nights
shows terrific his rage unmatched,
hatred and murder. To Hrothgar I
in greatness of soul would comfort bring.'

'March, then,' cried the watchman.
'Bear your weapons dearly on the path
I show you and I will bid my men to guard
your boat for fear lest foemen come.'
They bent them to march, the boat lay still,
fettered by cable and fast at anchor,
broad-bosomed ship. Then shone the boars
over the cheek-guard; chased with gold,
keen and gleaming, guard it kept

—

9

over the man of war, as marched along
heroes in haste, till the hall they saw,
broad of gable and bright with gold,
fairest of houses where Hrothgar ruled,
and the gleam of it lightened the lands afar.

V The Geats Reach Heorot

STONE-BRIGHT the street; it showed the way
to the crowd of Geats. On their shoulders bright
the steel rings sang, as they strode along
in mail of battle, and marched to the hall.
There, weary of ocean, along the wall
they set their broad shields down,
the breastplates clanged, war-gear of men;
their weapons stacked, spears stood together,
grey-tipped ash. Hrothgar's herald
asked of the heroes their home and kin.
'Why carry you burnished shields,
harness grey and helmets grim,
spears in multitude? Heroes so many
never met I as strangers of mood so strong.'
Proud earl of the Geats answer made,
hardy beneath helmet 'I am Beowulf named.
seeking Hrothgar.'

VI Beowulf Meets Hrothgar

HROTHGAR, white-haired and old,
with his earls about, cried 'Blessed God,'
at the sight of Beowulf and his men.
'This man hath been sent to slay
the night horror of Grendel. I hope to give
the good youth gold for his brave thought.
Welcome hither from over the sea!
You may wend your way in war-attire

and helmets for I, Hrothgar, greet you;
but let here the battle-shields bide your parley,
and wooden war-shafts wait its end.'

Strode forward the mighty one with his men,
brave band of thanes till the hearth they neared.
Beowulf spoke, his breastplate gleamed,
war-net woven by wit of the smith:
'Hrothgar, hail! Fame a plenty
have I gained in youth! These Grendel-deeds
I heard in my homeland heralded clear.
Seafarers say how stands this hall,
empty and idle, when evening sun
in the harbour of heaven is hidden away.
Same seafarers have seen me from slaughter come
blood-flecked from foes, where five I drowned,
and that wild brood the worst. In the waves I slew
water-goblins by night, in need and peril
avenging the Geats, whose woe they sought,
crushing the grim ones. Grendel now,
monster cruel, be mine to quell
in single battle! So, with this hardy band,
we will Heorot purge! Yet I hear, that monster dire,
in his wanton mood, of weapons uses not;
hence shall I scorn armour or sword
to bear in the fight, but with grip alone
must I confront the fiend and fight for life,
foe against foe. Then faith be his in the judgement
of the Lord whom death shall take.

'Yet if he win, in this hall of gold, my Geatish band
will he fearless eat, as oft before. My head,
will be dyed in gore, if death must take me
 then my blood-covered body he'll bear as prey,
and ruthless devour it, the roamer-lonely,
with my life-blood I'll redden his lair in the fen!

———

If defeated, to Hygelac send the armour which now guards
my chest, and tell my uncle, the King of the Geats,
that my bones with Grendel rest.'

VII Hrothgar Gives Advice

HROTHGAR spoke: 'Fight bravely, my Beowulf,
in Heorot Grendel with hate hath brought death.
Few now are my war-band for he
has wasted my hall-troop with deeds too dire.
And other earls with many armed men,
boasted often, as my mead they drank,
that they would stay in the mead-hall here,
and kill Grendel with their sharpened blades.
Then, when daylight broke, this mead-house
floor was covered with bone and gore,
blood splashed were boards and benches,
bloody was the hall. There are few heroes left,
but I ask you to sit for the feast, unbind thy words,
hardy hero, and give an old man comfort
as thy heart shall prompt thee.'

Gathered together, the Geatish men,
on bench assigned, sat down sturdy-hearted.
Hrothgar's liegemen then attended,
carried the carved cup with steady hand,
and willingly poured the gleaming mead.
The warriors sang, rejoiced together.
Hearty songs in Heorot. The heroes revelled,
proud and exultant were Geats and Dane,
and through wetted lips flowed words of courage.

VIII Unferth Taunts Beowulf

UNFERTH, the son of Ecglaf, sitting
at the feet of the Scyldings' lord, spoke.

Beowulf's quest sorely galled him
and ever did Unferth envy other men
able to achieve more in middle-earth
of fame under heaven than he himself.
'Art thou that Beowulf, Breca's rival,
who swam the open sea, and wantonly dared
in waters deep, to risk your life in a race?
Ocean-tides with your arms ye covered,
with strenuous hands the sea-streets measured.
Storms rolled rough waves, but in the realm of the sea,
Breca, it is said, outdid you entirely.
Breca beat thee, in strength excelled thee.
In seven nights his boast achieved,
Breca, it was, who tasted victory.
So, brave Beowulf, are you not afraid
that Grendel will outdo you? Dare you even
wait through the night for the monster?'

Beowulf spoke, son of Ecgtheow:
'What a great deal hast thou uttered,
Unferth, drunken with mead.
Of Breca now, it was his triumph.
Though in truth I claim that I have had
more success in the sea than any man else,
more ocean-endurance. We made our boast
in time of youth to stake our lives
far at sea: and so we performed it.
Naked swords, as we swam along,
we held in hand, with hope to guard us
against the whales. Not a yard from me
could he float afar; nor him I abandoned.
Together for five nights full till the sea
divided us, churning waves, coldest weather,
darkling night, and the northern wind
ruthless rushed on us: rough was the surge.
Now the wrath of the sea-beasts rose apace;

and one hateful monster grasped me firm
and, with grimmest grip, dragged me down.
I pierced the monster with point of sword,
with blade of battle: huge beast of the sea
was overwhelmed by hand of mine.

IX Beowulf Silences Unferth

'Oft the evil serpent monsters thronging
threatened me, but with thrust of my sword,
my faithful sword, I dealt them due return!
No chance had they to devour their victim,
vengeful creatures, no seated banquet
had they at the bottom of sea; but by break of day
they lay, asleep by my sword. And since,
by them on the fathomless sea, sailors
are never molested. Light from east,
came bright God's beacon; the billows sank,
so that I saw the sea-cliffs high,
windy walls. For God often saveth
earl undoomed if he resilient be!
And so it came that I killed with my sword
nine of the monsters. Of night-fought battles
never heard I a harder battle beneath heaven,
and though spent with swimming, the sea upbore me.
And so I say, Unferth, son of Ecglaf,
slayer of brothers and cold-blooded killer,
never would have Grendel these grim deeds wrought,
monster dire, on thy master dear, if damned heart
of thine were as battle-bold as thy boast is loud!
Grendel thinks him safe, from such Scyldings,
and lustily murders, fights and feasts.
But speedily now shall I prove to him
the prowess and pride of the Geats.
I shall bid him battle and tomorrow,
when light of dawn breaks, will we feast.'

Joyous was Hrothgar, the grey-haired,
war-famed bountiful giver of treasure,
to hear from Beowulf such firm resolve.
Then was laughter of liegemen loud resounding
with winsome words. Wealhtheow came forth,
queen of Hrothgar, heedful of courtesy,
gold-decked, greeting the guests in hall;
and the high-born lady handed the cup
first to her husband, battle-famed king,
who bade her sing at the mead-carousing.

Through the hall then went the Scyldings' Lady,
to younger and older everywhere
she carried the cup, till come the moment
when the ring-graced queen, the royal-hearted,
to Beowulf bore the beaker of mead.
She greeted the Geats' lord, God she thanked,
in wisdom's words, that her will was granted,
that at last on a hero her hope could lean
for comfort in terrors. The cup he took,
hardy-in-war, from Wealhtheow's hand,
and answer uttered the eager-for-combat.

Beowulf spoke, son of Ecgtheow:
'This was my thought, when my thanes and I
bent to the ocean and entered our boat,
that I would work the will of your people
fully, or in fighting fall in death,
in fiend's grip fast. I am firm to do
an earl's brave deed, or end the days
of this life of mine in the mead-hall here.'
Well these words to the woman seemed,
Beowulf's battle-boast. Bright with gold
the stately dame by her husband sat.

Again, as before, began in the hall

warriors' wassail and words of power,
till presently Unferth hastened to seek
rest for the night; he knew there waited
fight for the fiend in that festal hall,
when the shine of the sun they saw no more.
And dusk of night began to thicken,
and shadowy shapes came striding on.
The warriors rose and Hrothgar to Beowulf,
bade him farewell and a word he added:
'Never to any man before I trusted,
since I could heave up sword and shield,
this noble Dane-Hall, till now to thee.
Have now and hold this house unpeered;
remember thy glory; thy might declare;
watch for the monster! No wish shall fail thee
if you win the battle with brave-won life.'

X All Sleep Except One

THEN Hrothgar went with his men attending,
defence-of-Scyldings, forth from hall.
He set a guard against Grendel,
so heroes heard, a hall-defender,
who watched for the shadow monster.
In truth, the Geats' Beowulf gladly trusted
his mettle, his might, the mercy of God!
Cast off then his chainmail of iron,
helmet from head; to his henchman gave,
choicest of weapons, the well-chased sword,
bidding him guard the gear of battle.
Spoke Beowulf before the bed be sought:
'Not I with sword-edge to sooth him to slumber,
though well I am able to chop and cleave him,
no skill is his to strike against me.
We both, this night shall spurn the sword.
If he seek me here I'll be unweaponed for war

and let wisest God decree victory as he sees fit.'

Reclined then our hero, and pillows held
the head of the earl, while all about him
his weary men on hall-beds sank.
None of them thought that thence their steps
to the land they loved, would lead them back!
Full well they knew how slaughter had snatched
so many in the banquet-hall of Danish clan.
But comfort and help their Master gave, though
through the cold night-mist striding,
came the walker-in-shadow, the ghostly ravager.
Warriors slept whose task was to guard the hall,
all save one: wakeful, ready, with warrior's wrath,
bold he waited the battle's issue.

XI Grendel Comes from the Fens

THEN from the moorland, by misty crags,
with God's wrath laden, Grendel came.
The monster was minded of mankind now
some to seize in the stately mead-house.
Under the waning moon he walked, till
gold-hall of men, he gladly discerned,
flashing with fretwork. Not first time, this,
that he the home of Hrothgar sought,
yet never in his life-day, late or early,
such hardy heroes, such hall-thanes, found!
To the house the demon walked apace,
parted from peace; with fists and fingers
he beat and tore at the door. Forged bolts
failed to hold fast. With bitter fury he burst
into the hall, ranged furiously over the paved floor.
With bloodlust the fiend strode; fearful flashes
streamed from his eyes, like flame to see.

He spied in hall the hero-band,
kin and clansmen clustered asleep,
hardy liegemen. Then laughed his heart;
for the monster was minded, before dawn,
to savage and sever the soul of each,
take life from body, since lusty banquet
waited his will! But fate that night
had dealt him a fairer match.

Beowulf eagerly watched his gruesome foe.
How would he fare in forthcoming fight?
Not that the monster was minded to pause!
Straightway he seized a sleeping warrior
the first to suffer, and tore him fiercely asunder,
the bone-frame bit, drank blood in streams,
swallowed him in mouthfuls: swiftly thus
the lifeless corpse was clear devoured,
even feet and hands.

Nearer Grendel strode till, with fiendish claw,
he grasped Beowulf, the silent warrior.
The hero, on elbow resting, was lifted boldly,
but the stout-hearted are prompt to answer,
when caught by the night's damned riser.
Soon then discovered that shepherd-of-evils
that none in this haunted middle-world,
has as strong a handgrip as our fair warrior.
Bethought Beowulf, hardy Hygelac-thane,
of his boast at evening, and grasped firm his foe.

At heart Grendel feared, sorrowed in soul,
wanted to escape! Anxious to flee,
his darkness seek, the den of devils.
No doings now as often done in days of old!
The fiend tried to make off, but our hero held firm.
The monster meant - if he might at all -

to fling himself free, and far away
fly to the fens, knew the fingers' power
in the grip of a determined one.
Din filled the room; Grendel's cries echoed,
in the ears of castle-dwellers and clansmen far.
Wonder it was the mead-hall stood firm
with the strain of their struggle. To earth
the fair house fell not; too fast it was
within and without by its iron bands
craftily clamped; though there crashed
many a bench where the grim foes wrestled.
Again uprose hymns of howling horror.
Danes of the North were filled with fear
as through the walls the wailing sorrow
flew through the biting air, Again and again
God's hell-bound foe sang his grisly song,
cry of the conquered, cry of clamorous pain.

XII Grendel is Vanquished

WITH the hateful hell-bringer captive
in Beowulf's pitiless hand, the Geats
would not suffer Grendel to live.
Deeming useless his days and years
to men on earth, now many a brave
thane, brandishing blade ancestral,
rushed to Beowulf's side. Yet these
hardy-hearted heroes of war, aiming
their swords, with keenest blade,
failed to harm that hideous fiend!
He was safe, by his spells, from edge of iron,
though his parting woeful would be.
Harmful in heart and hated of God,
the frame of his body would fail him now.
Beowulf, the keen-souled kinsman of Hygelac
still held him by the hand; hateful alive

was each to other. The direful demon
took mortal hurt; a mighty wound
showed on his shoulder. Sinews shivered,
snapped, his bone-frame burst,
and the loathsome was limb torn asunder.
To Beowulf the glory was given, and Grendel,
now death-sick, sought his den in the dark moor,
evil, dank abode: he knew too well
that here was the last of life, an end
to his bloody days and nights on earth.
The slaughter was over and victory
fell to the thanes, for they had rescued
Hrothgar's hall from the roving stranger.
Beowulf, the valiant Geat, had kept his pledge
which had been given to the Eastern Danes.
No more were they to suffer the soul-crushing
sorrow from the battle they had borne for so long.
Proof of this was Grendel's arm, shoulder, and claw,
which Beowulf suspended in the gabled hall.

XIII Rejoicing of the Danes

MANY warriors, from far and near, gathered
round the hall, the wonder to see at dawn:
the arm of the traitor. Not troublesome seemed
the monster's end to any man
who saw by the graceless foe's foot tracks
how the weary demon, had made his way
from Heorot. Steps, death-marked, dragged
themselves to the devil's fen where
bloody currents were boiling there,
and thick the tide of tumbling waves,
water by that doomed one dyed, who on
the moor laid forlorn his life down,
his heathen soul, and hell received it.

Home then rode the fur-clad clansmen
from that merry journey, and many a youth,
on horses white, the hardy warriors,
came back from the moor. Then Beowulf's glory
eager they echoed, and all agreed
that from sea to sea, from south to north,
there was no other in earth's domain,
under vault of heaven, more valiant found,
of warriors none more worthy to rule!
(On their lord beloved they laid no slight,
gracious Hrothgar: a good king he!)
Of Beowulf's quest the bard sang,
and artfully added an excellent tale,
in well-ranged words, of the warlike deeds
he had heard in the saga of Sigemund,
slayer of a dragon, protector of a golden hoard.

XIV Hrothgar's Gratitude

HROTHGAR spoke on the hall steps
clutching Grendel's hand: 'To our Sovereign
a speedy thanks for the sight we see.
A throng of sorrows I have borne from Grendel;
but God still works wonder on wonder.
This hero now, Beowulf, a work has done
that not all of us could ever do
by guile and wisdom. Lo, well can she say
whosoever of women this warrior bore
among sons of men, if still she liveth,
that the God of the ages was good to her
in the birth of her bairn. Now, Beowulf, thee,
of heroes best, I shall heartily love
as mine own, my son; preserve thou ever
this kinship new: thou shalt never lack
wealth of the world that I wield as mine!
Full oft for less have I largess showered,

my precious hoard, on a weaker man,
less stout in struggle. Thyself hast now
fulfilled such deeds, that thy fame shall endure
through all the ages. As ever he did,
well may fate reward thee still!'

Beowulf spoke, son of Ecgtheow:
'This work of war most willingly
we have fought, though when in strongest grip
I wished to bind Grendel down, that here
would be his bed of death where he should
breathe his last: but he broke away.
Too sturdy was he, keen in running!
For rescue, however, he left behind
his hand in pledge, arm and shoulder;
yet no longer he liveth, loathsome fiend,
sunk in his sins, and sorrow holds him
tightly grasped in grip of anguish.'

Silent was Unferth, son of Ecglaf,
since athelings all beheld that hand,
on the high roof hanging: demon's fingers,
with sturdy nails like steel, a heathen's hand-spear,
hostile warrior's claws uncanny. 'Twas clear,'
others said, 'that no blade could ever sever
the battle-hand from such an ungodly monster.'

XV Hrothgar Lavishes Gifts upon his Deliverer

THERE was hurry in Heorot now
for men and women the mead-hall to cleanse,
the guest-room to garnish. Brightly shone the hangings
that were woven on the wall, and wonders many
to delight each mortal that looks upon them.
Hrothgar himself would sit to banquet
and Heorot now was filled with friends.

To brave Beowulf the mighty king gave
a golden banner, symbol of triumph was the
embroidered battle-flag, breastplate and helmet;
and a splendid sword by many was seen
borne to the fearless one. Beowulf took
cup in hall: for such costly gifts
he suffered no shame in the warriors' throng.
For few heroes, in heartier mood,
with four such gifts, so fashioned with gold,
on the ale-bench honoured others thus!
Then Hrothgar bade his men lead
horses eight, with carven head-gear,
adown the hall: one steed was decked
with a saddle all shining and set in jewels;
'twas the battle-seat of the best of kings.
Both were brought over to Beowulf,
and, with war-steeds and weapons,
they wished him joy of them.
Gold for the slayer of Grendel was then
the price Hrothgar bade his warriors pay.
And an heirloom the Scyldings gave,
to each Geat that came over the briny way.

XVI The Banquet Continues

COMES Wealhtheow forth, the Scylding queen
to speak: 'My king and lord, treasure-bestower,
joy attend thee, gold-friend of heroes,
and, my kind ruler, be glad with thy Geats.
Our golden Heorot is purged, enjoy
while thou canst, but think on thy kin
before thou goest to greet thy doom.
For gracious I deem our son Hrothmund,
willing to hold and rule, if thou yield up first,
king of Scyldings, thy part in the world.'

Then she turned to Beowulf and a beaker
she gave him, with kindly greeting,
of wounded gold, to honour him, then arm-rings,
chest-plate and collars of the noblest kind.
A hoard of gems for Beowulf, the hero.
Wealhtheow then spoke amid the warriors:
'This jewel enjoy in thy jocund youth,
preserve thy strength, and to son of mine
counsel in kindness and be helpful in deed.
Here every earl to the other is true,
mild of mood, to the master loyal!
Thanes are friendly, the throng obedient,
liegemen are revelling: listen and obey!'
Wealhtheow then returned to her place
while mead flowed for the warriors.

Fate they knew not, destiny dire,
and the doom to be seen by many
when darkling evening should come.
Hrothgar homeward hastened away,
royal, to rest. The room was guarded
by an army of men, as before was done.
They bared the bench-boards; abroad they spread
their blankets. One mead-carouser,
doomed unto death, lay down in the hall.
At their heads they set their shields of war,
and swords bright; on the bench were their
high battle-helmets, their haughty spears.
'Twas ever their custom to be ready for battle.

XVII The Mother of Grendel

THEN sank they to sleep. With sorrow they bought
their rest of the evening, as often time had happened
when Grendel raided that golden hall,
evil he brought, till his end drew nigh,

slaughter for sins. Yet one avenger survived the fiend,
as was learned afar. The livelong time
after that grim fight, Grendel's mother,
monster of women, mourned her woe.
She was doomed to dwell in the dreary waters,
cold sea-courses, since Cain cut down
with edge of the sword his only brother,
his father's offspring: outlawed he fled,
marked with murder, from men's delights
hid in the wilds. There woke from him
such fate-sent ghosts as Grendel, who,
war-wolf horrid, at Heorot found
Beowulf watching and waiting the fray,
with whom the grisly one grappled amain.
But the man remembered his mighty power,
the glorious gift that God had sent him,
in his Maker's mercy put his trust
for comfort and help: so he conquered the foe,
felled the fiend, who fled abject,
bereft of joy, to the realms of death,
mankind's foe. And his mother now,
gloomy and grim, would go on the quest
of sorrow, the death of her son to avenge.

To Heorot came she, devil-shaped woman,
where Danes slept in the hall. Too soon returned
old ills of the thanes, when in she burst,
the mother of Grendel. Less grim,
as terror of woman in war is less
than of men in arms, yet she carried her woe,
was full of vengeance for the death of her son.
Then, spied in the night shade, the hard-edge
is quickly drawn and shields a-many
firm held in hand; not helmet minded
nor harness of mail, whom that horror gripped.
Haste was hers; a single atheling up she seized

fast and firm, before she fled to the moor.
He was for Hrothgar of heroes the dearest,
whom she killed on his couch, a clansman famous,
in battle brave. Nor was Beowulf there;
another house had been held apart,
after giving of gold, for the Geat renowned.

Uproar filled Heorot; Grendel's hand
all blood-flecked, she bore with her,
her grief renewed; misery has returned.
Long-tried Hrothgar at heart was sad
when he knew his noble no more lived,
and dead indeed was his dearest thane.
As daylight broke, the Geats were brought
in haste to the king, and Beowulf asked
if the night had passed in peace.

XVIII Hrothgar's Account of Monsters

HROTHGAR spoke: 'Ask not of peace!
Grief has returned to Danish folk.
Dead is Aeschere, my sage adviser,
shoulder-comrade when fighting in battle,
when warriors clashed we guarded our heads,
my noble hero, my wise friend.
But here in Heorot a hand hath slain him,
an avenging death-sprite unyielding.
Grendel in grimmest grasp thou killed.
Now another comes, keen and cruel,
her kin to avenge, faring far in feud of blood.
Land-dwellers I have heard relate
that such a pair they have sometimes seen,
march-stalkers mighty, the moorland haunting,
wandering spirits: one of them seemed,
so far as my folk could fairly judge,
of womankind; and one, accursed,

in man's guise trod the misery-track
of exile, though huger than human bulk.
Grendel they named him; his father they knew not,
nor any brood that was born to him
of treacherous spirits. Untrod is their home;
by wolf-cliffs haunt they and windy headlands,
fenways fearful, where flows the stream
from mountains gliding to gloom beneath rocks
in underground flood. Not far is it hence
in measure of miles that the moor expands,
and over it the frost-bound forest hanging,
sturdily rooted, shadows their cliff.
Even the hounded deer, harried by dogs,
will not seek refuge in such an uncanny place.
'Tis no happy land where winds bestir
evil storms and the heavens weep.

'Now your help, Beowulf, once more is needed.
The land thou knowst not, this place of fear,
but there will thou findest out
that sin-flecked being. Seek if thou dare!
I will reward thee, for waging this fight,
with ancient treasure, as before I did,
with shining gold, if thou emerges victorious.'

XIX Beowulf Seeks Grendel's Mother

BEOWULF spoke: 'Sorrow not. 'Tis better
to avenge friends than fruitlessly mourn them.
Rise, O King! Ride we anon, and let us hasten
to mark the trail of the mother of Grendel.
Endure this day with patience, but no harbour
shall hide her, let her flee where she will.
Heed my promise, we will find her!'

For Hrothgar soon a horse was saddled

and with Beowulf the sovereign wise
stately rode on; his shield-armed men
followed in force. The footprints led
along the woodland, widely seen,
a path over the plain, where she passed, and trod
the murky moor; over stone-cliffs steep,
narrow passes and unknown ways,
headlands sheer, and the haunts of water demons.
Foremost Hrothgar fared, Beowulf at his side,
till he found in a flash the forested hill
hanging over the hoary rock,
a woeful wood: the waves below
were dyed in blood. The Danish men
had sorrow of soul and for many a hero
'twas hard to bear, when Aeschere's head
they found by the flood on the foreland there.
Waves were welling, the warriors saw,
hot with blood; but the horn often sang
battle-song bold. The band sat down,
and watched on the water worm-like things,
sea-dragons strange that sounded the deep,
and sea-snakes that lay on the ledge.
These started away, swollen and savage,
at the war-horn's blast.

Fearless Beowulf, with bolt from bow,
shot a war-shaft at one monster, amid its heart
went the keen arrow; with boar-spears well
hooked and barbed, it was hard beset,
done to death and dragged on the headland,
wave-roamer wondrous. Warriors viewed
the grisly guest. Then prepared himself,
Beowulf, in martial mail. His breastplate broad
and bright of hues, his helmet too,
worked by a weapon-smith with boars set in,
was destined to dare the deeps of the flood.

Hrothgar's orator, Unferth, offered 'Hrunting'
a hilted sword, of heirlooms easily first;
iron was its edge, all etched with poison,
with battle-blood hardened. Not for the first time
was it destined to do a daring task.
For Unferth bore not in mind the speech
he had made, drunk with mead. This weapon
he lent to a stouter swordsman, one now
armed and ready for his grim encounter.

XX Beowulf Fights with Grendel's Mother

BEOWULF spoke: 'Have mind what once was said,
if in thy cause it came that I should lose my life,
thou, Hrothgar, wouldst be guardian to my thanes
and the gifts thou gavest me to Hygelac send.
And let Unferth wield this wondrous sword,
far-honoured, this heirloom precious,
hard of edge: with Hrunting I shall
gain more glory, or Death shall take me.'
After these words Beowulf boldly hastened,
and the waves swallowed the hero. Long
the day passed before he saw the sea floor.

Soon realised the fiend in her grisly domain
that some guest from above, some man,
was raiding her monster-realm.
She grasped out for him with horrible claws,
and seized the warrior; yet unscathed was
his body; the shining breastplate hindered,
as she strove to shatter the bark of war,
the linked harness from loathsome hand.
Then the sea-wolf bore the hero down
to the lair she haunted while vainly he strove,
his weapon to wield against wondrous monsters
that sore beset him; sea-beasts many

tried with fierce tusks to tear his mail,
and swarmed on the noble stranger.

But soon Beowulf marked the shining walls
of some dark cavern, he knew not which,
where water could work him no harm,
nor through the roof could reach him ever
storm or flood. Firelight he saw,
beams of a blaze that brightly shone.
Then the warrior was aware of mere-maid
monstrous. A mighty stroke he swung his blade,
yet the blow cleaved not. Instead, sang on her head
that seemly blade its war-song wild.
But the warrior found the sword was loath
to bite, to harm the heart: its hard edge failed
the noble at need. First time, this,
for the gleaming blade to fail.
Firm Beowulf stood, not lacking in valour.
He flung away the fretted sword
and on rocky floor it lay, steel-edged and stiff.
His strength he trusted, handgrip of might.
So man, reckless of living, will do whatever
is required to gain him battle-glory unending.

Seizing then the sea-hag by her shoulder,
he shrank not from combat but, filled with wrath,
flung Grendel's fierce mother to the ground.
Swift on her part she paid him back
with ungodly grasp, and grappled with him.
Soon spent with struggle, stumbled the warrior,
fiercest of fighting-men, and tumbled down.
On the intruder she hurled herself,
wielded her war-knife, broad and brown-edged,
the bairn to avenge, her sole-born son.
On Beowulf's shoulder lay braided breast-mail,
barring death, withstanding entrance of edge or blade.

Life would have ended for Ecgtheow's son,
beneath the earth, had his armour not aided him,
battle-net hard, and had God not fought for his cause.

XXI Beowulf Fights On

AMID the battle-gear in the sea-hag's cavern
Beowulf saw a blade triumphant, an ancient
giant sword edged with proof as a warrior's
heirloom, weapon unmatched, larger than any man,
as if the giants had wrought it, ready and keen.
Seizing then its hilt, bold and battle-grim,
he brandished the sword and, with a wrathful
stroke, plunged it into her neck; heard her bones
breaking. The blade pierced through that fated-one's
flesh and to floor she unwillingly sank.
Bloody the blade and faint was he after the deed.
Then blazed forth light. 'Twas bright within
as when from the sky there shines unclouded
heaven's candle. The rocks he scanned.
By the wall then went he; his weapon raised
in search of Grendel, to give the monster requital
for the grim raids many, for those he slew
in slumber, in sleep devoured. Grendel he saw,
spent with war, spoiled of life, wounded
from Heorot's battle. The body sprang far
when after death it endured the blow,
sword-stroke savage, that severed its head.

Hrothgar's companions saw the surging waters
with wine-blood blooming. Old men spoke together,
Beowulf would not come again to seek
their mighty master. To many it seemed
the wicked sea-wolf had won his life.
The ninth hour came. The noble Scyldings
left the headland; homeward went

the gold-friend of men. But the Geats sat on,
stared at the surges, soul-sick, sorrowful,
wanting to see their lord again.

Beowulf's sword, from blood of the fight,
began to shrivel, to melt like ice. Treasure lay
round him, but he took nothing more than
Grendel's head and the sword's handle,
blazoned with jewels; the blade had withered,
burned was the bright sword, her blood was so hot,
so poisoned the hell-sprite who perished within there.
Soon he was swimming, up through the flood.
The clashing waters were cleansed now,
of the wandering fiend, her life-days done,
and through the cold, lapping world,
swam then Beowulf to land, the sailors' refuge,
sturdy-in-spirit, of sea-booty glad,
of burden brave he bore with him.
Went his thanes to greet him, thanking God
for his safe return. Soon helmet and armour
were loosened while the blood-stained sea
crashed upon the rocks and sand.
Forth they fared by the footpaths thence,
merry at heart the highways measured,
well-known roads. Four courageous men
carried Grendel's head on a spear, an arduous
task, and on the shaft-of-slaughter they bore it
to the hall. Fourteen Geats, marching came.
Beowulf, mighty amid them, the meadow-ways trod;
fearless in fight, of fame renowned,
hardy hero, Hrothgar to greet.
And next by the hair into hall was borne
Grendel's head, an awe to clan and queen alike,
a monster of marvel for one and all.

XXII Beowulf Brings his Trophies

BEOWULF spoke: 'Lo, now, this sea-booty,
Lord of Scyldings, we've lustily brought thee,
sign of glory; thou seest it here.
Not lightly did I with my life escape!
In war under water this work I achieved
with endless effort and the Lord to defend me.
Not a whit could I with Hrunting do
in work of war, though the weapon is good;
yet a sword I spied, in splendour hanging,
old, gigantic, and I fought with that blade,
felling in fight, since fate was with me,
the wards of the cavern. That war-sword then
all burned, bright blade, when the blood gushed o'er it,
battle-sweat hot; but the hilt I brought back
from my foes. So avenged I their fiendish deeds,
as was due and right. And this is my promise,
that in Heorot now safe thou can sleep
and every thane of all thy folk both old and young;
no evil fear from that side again.'

Then the golden hilt, for Hrothgar,
that grey-haired leader, in hand was laid.
This he viewed, heirloom old, handle of shining gold.
In runic letters it was rightly said for whom
the serpent-traced sword was wrought,
best of blades, in bygone days. Hrothgar spoke:
'So, thy fame must fly, O friend my Beowulf,
far and wide o'er folksteads many.
Love of mine will I assure thee, as, awhile ago,
I promised; thou shalt prove a friend in future,
in far-off years, to folk of thine, to the heroes a help.
Beowulf, best of men, profit eternal, yet temper thy pride,
The flower of thy might lasts now a while, but before long
it shall be that sickness or sword or brandished spear

33

or odious age thy strength shall diminish.
Death, even thee, in haste shall overwhelm.
The Ring-Danes these fifty years I have ruled,
protected them bravely from mighty-ones,
from spear and sword, till it seemed for me
no foe could be found under fold of the sky.
Lo, sudden the shift! To me seated secure
came grief for joy when Grendel began
to harry my home, the hellish foe;
for those ruthless raids, unresting I suffered
heart-sorrow heavy. Heaven be thanked,
Lord Eternal, for life extended
that I with eyes may gaze on Grendel's head
all hewn and bloody, after long evil.
Go to the bench now. Be glad at banquet,
warrior worthy! A wealth of treasure
at dawn of day, be dealt between us.'

Glad was the Geats' lord, going betimes
to seek his seat, as the king commanded.
All feasted until night was fixed when
aged Scylding and wander-weary Geat,
for sleeping yearned. So slumbered the stout-heart
till a black raven came flying, shine after shadow,
and heralded the dawn. The swordsmen hastened,
Geats all were eager homeward forth to fare;
and far from thence the great-hearted guest
would guide his boat's keel. The sword Hrunting
was given to Beowulf, the sword Unferth bade him take,
excellent iron. He uttered his thanks for it,
and counted it keen in battle, with words
he slandered not the edge of the blade.

XXIII Sorrow at Parting

BEOWULF spoke: 'We seafarers will say

our farewell, that we leave to seek
Hygelac now. We here have found
hosts to our heart: thou hast harboured us well.
If ever on earth I am able to win me
more of thy love from work of war
I am willing still. If it come to me ever
across the seas that enemies flood thy shores,
thousands of thanes shall I bring, heroes to help thee.'

Him then answering, Hrothgar spoke:
'No wiser counsel from so young in years
ever yet have I heard. Thou art strong
and in mind art wary, art wise in words.
No seemlier man will the Sea-Geats find
at all to choose for their chief and king,
for hoard-guard of heroes, if hold thou wilt
thy kinsman's kingdom! Thy keen mind pleases me
the longer the better, Beowulf loved!
Thou hast brought it about that both our peoples,
sons of the Geat and Spear-Dane folk,
shall have mutual peace, and from murderous strife,
such as once they waged, from war refrain.
Long as I rule this realm so wide,
let our hoards be common, let heroes with gold
greet each other over the gannet's-bath,
and the ringed-ships bear over rolling waves
tokens of love. I pledge my landfolk
towards friend and foe are firmly joined,
and honour they keep in the olden way.'
To him in the hall, then, Hrothgar
gave treasures twelve, and bade him fare
safely with the gifts back to his home.
Then kissed the king and fast flowed the tears
of the grey-headed. Heavy with winters,
he clung to this, that each should look
on the other again and hear him in hall.

Then Beowulf strode, glad of his gold-gifts,
towards the wave-roamer riding at anchor.
As they hastened onward, Hrothgar's gifts
they praised at length. 'Twas a lord unpeered,
every way blameless, a worthy, generous king.

XXIV The Homeward Journey

THE watchman on the coast marked,
trusty as ever, the Geats' return.
From the height of the hill no hostile words
reached the guests as he rode to greet them;
but 'Welcome!' he called to that brave clan.
Then on the sand, with steeds and treasure
and armour their broad and roomy ship
was heavily laden: high its mast
rose over Hrothgar's hoarded gems.
A sword to the watchman Beowulf gave,
mounted with gold. Their ocean-vessel boarding,
they drove through the deep, and Daneland left.

A sea-cloth was set, a sail with ropes,
firm to the mast; the sea-timbers moaned;
the craft sped on, foam-necked it floated forth
over the waves, over the green swelling sea,
till they came in sight of the Geatish cliffs,
home-known headlands. High the boat,
stirred by winds, on the sand updrove.

Helpful at haven the harbour-guard stood,
who long already for loved companions
by the water had waited and watched afar.
He bound to the beach the broad-bosomed ship
with anchor-bands, lest ocean-billows
that trusty timber should tear away.
Then Beowulf bade them bear the treasure,

gold and jewels; no journey far
was it thence to go to the giver of rings,
King Hygelac: at home he dwelt with his queen,
Hygd, by the sea-wall close, himself and his clan.
Haughty that house, a hero the king,
high the hall with a queen right young,
wise and wary, though few winters
she had spent in those fortress walls.
Nor humble her ways, nor grudged she gifts
to the Geatish men of precious treasure.

XXV Beowulf and Hygelac

HASTENED Beowulf the sandy strand
of the sea to tread. The world's great candle
shone from the south. They strode along
with sturdy steps to the spot they knew
where the battle-king shared the rings,
shelter-of-heroes. To King Hygelac
Beowulf's coming was quickly told,
and with haste in the hall, room for the rovers
was readily made. By his king he sat,
come safe from battle, kinsman by kinsman.
His kindly lord he first had greeted in gracious form,
with manly words. The mead dispensing,
came through the high hall, young Queen Hygd
charming to warriors, wine-cup she bore
to the hands of the heroes. Hygelac then
his comrade fairly with question plied
in the lofty hall, sore longing to know
what manner of stay the Sea-Geats had made.
'What came of thy quest, my kinsman Beowulf?
Poor King Hrothgar couldst thou aid at all?
Long I begged thee by no means to seek
that slaughtering monster, but suffer the Danes
to settle their feud themselves with Grendel.

Yet God be thanked that safe I see thee now!'

Beowulf spoke: 'Tis known and unhidden,
the struggle grim between Grendel and me,
which we fought on the field where full too many
sorrows he wrought. These all I avenged.
But first I went to Hrothgar to greet in the hall
to put my purpose plain to him. They received us
tenderly. Often to their visitors Hrothgar's Queen
and his lovely daughter the mead-cup tendered.
But I pass from that, turning to Grendel,
at night that fierce sprite came to seek us out
where safe and sound we sentried the hall.
A warrior first was slain, Grendel on him
turned murderous mouth, on our mighty kinsman,
and all of the brave man's body devoured.
Yet never more the bloody-toothed murderer
would return to Hrothgar's gold-decked hall:
for me he grasped, caught in terror of might.
'Twere long to relate how that land-destroyer
I paid in kind for his cruel deeds;
yet there, my prince, this people of thine
got fame by my fighting. He fled away,
and a little space his life preserved;
but there staid behind him his stronger hand
left in Heorot; heartsick thence
on the floor of the ocean that outcast fell.
Me for this struggle the Scyldings' friend
paid in plenty with plates of gold,
with many a treasure, when morn had come
and we all at the banquet-board sat down.
Then was song and glee. The grey-haired Scylding,
much tested, told of the times of yore.
Thus in the hall the whole of that day
at ease we feasted, till darkest night.

'Anon full ready in greed of vengeance,
Grendel's mother set forth. Dead was her son
through the wrath of Geats; now, woman monstrous
with fury fell upon a Dane, avenged her offspring,
an agèd advisor she slew. When morning broke,
those Danish folk mourned the death of the man.
Under mountain stream she had carried the corpse.
For Hrothgar that was the heaviest sorrow.
The sad king then, by thy life, besought me
to play the hero and hazard my being
for glory of prowess. I then entered the waters,
'tis widely known, and the sea-hag found.
Hand-to-hand there a while we struggled;
billows welled blood; in the briny hall
her head I hewed with a hardy blade
and gained my life, though not without danger.
My doom was not yet. Then generous Hrothgar
gave me great gifts of honourable worth.
But to thee, my prince, I proffer them all,
gladly give them. Thy grace alone
can find me favour. Few indeed
have I of kinsmen, save thee, King Hygelac.'

Then Beowulf bade them bear to the king
the boar-head standard, the battle-helm high,
breastplate iron-grey and splendid sword.
The necklace to young Hygd, Beowulf presented,
which Wealhtheow had given him. The gem gleamed
bright on the breast of the queen. Three steeds
he added, slender and saddle-bright.
Thus Beowulf was praised for mighty deeds
and acts of honour. When carousing he slew not
comrade or kin; nor cruel his mood, though of sons
of earth his strength was greatest, a glorious gift
that God had sent the brave, splendid man.
Slack and shiftless the strong men had once

deemed Beowulf; but payment came,
to the warrior honoured, for all his woes.
Then Hygelac bade bring within a sword
garnished with gold: no Geat ever knew
in shape of such a weapon a statelier prize.
The sword he laid in Beowulf's lap;
and of acres assigned him several thousand,
with house and high-seat.

XXVI Beowulf Reigns

NOW further it fell with the flight of years,
with harryings horrid, that Hygelac perished,
and his son too, by hewing of swords.
Then Beowulf came as king this broad
realm to wield; and he ruled it well
fifty winters, a wise old prince,
warding his land, until a dragon began
in the dark of blackest night to rage.
In the grave on the hill a hoard it guarded,
in the stone-barrow steep. A strait path reached it,
unknown to mortals. Some man, however,
came by chance that cave within
to the heathen hoard. In hand he took
a golden goblet, nor gave he it back,
stole with it away, while the watcher slept,
by thievish wiles: for the dragon's wrath
prince and people must pay betimes!

XXVII The Hoard and the Dragon

THAT way the thief went with no will of his own,
in danger of life, to the dragon's hoard,
but for pressure of peril, he fled in fear
and seeking shelter, a sinful man,
entered in. At the awful sight

tottered that guest, and terror seized him;
yet the wretched fugitive rallied anon
from fright and fear before he fled away,
and took the cup from that treasure-hoard.

Of such besides there was store enough,
heirlooms old, the earth below,
which some earl forgotten, in ancient years,
the last of his lofty race, had hidden away,
dearest treasure. For death had hurried all hence;
and the earl alone left to live, the last of the clan,
weeping for his friends, yet wished to bide
warding the treasure, his one delight,
though brief his respite. The barrow, new-ready,
to sand and sea-waves stood anear,
hard by the headland, hidden and closed.
Few words the earl spoke: 'Now hold thou, earth,
since heroes may not, what I have owned!
Battle-death has seized my clansmen all,
robbed them of life and a liegeman's joys.
None have I left to lift the sword,
or to cleanse the carven cup of price,
beaker bright. My brave are gone.
And the helmet hard, all haughty with gold,
shall part from its plating. Polishers sleep
who could brighten and burnish the battle-mask;
and shields rust with their bearer. No hawk now
flies through the hall, nor horses fleet
stamp in readiness. Battle and death
the flower of my race have torn away.'
Mournful of mood, thus the earl moaned
his woe alone, and wept by day and night,
till death's fell wave overwhelmed his heart.

His hoard-of-bliss a dragon open found,
who, blazing at twilight, the folk of earth

sorely dreaded. Undisturbed he guarded
the treasure for three hundred winters;
till the thief aroused anger in his breast.
To his master the thief took the costly cup,
borne off was the booty. Forgiveness was granted
to that wretched man; and his ruler saw
first time what was fashioned in far-off days.
When the dragon awoke, new woe was kindled.
Over the stone he snuffed. The stark-heart found
footprint of foe who had crept silently
in his hidden craft by the creature's head.

That warden of gold over the ground went seeking,
keen to find the man who had wronged him in sleep.
Savage and burning, the barrow he circled.
War he desired, was eager for battle,
yet the serpent-guardian waited
ill-enduring till evening came;
boiling with wrath was the barrow's keeper,
and keen with flame the foe to pay
for the dear cup's loss. Now day was fled
as the serpent had wished. By its wall no more
was it glad to bide, but burning flew
high-folded in flame: a fearful beginning
for sons of the soil; and soon it came,
soaring doom-ladened, wings of dreadful note.

XXVIII The Dragon's Revenge

THEN the baleful fiend its fire belched out,
and bright homes burned. The blaze stood high
all land's folk fleeing. No living thing
would that loathly one leave as aloft it flew.
Wide was the dragon's warring seen,
its fiendish fury spent far and near.
The grim destroyer of the Geats,

42

hating and hounding and lapping in flame,
till at the first hint of dawn, it hastened
to its treasure hoard and hidden lair.

To Beowulf the sorry tale was told
quickly and truly: the king's own homestead,
of buildings the best, in flame-waves melted,
that gift-throne of Geats. To the good old man
sad in heart, 'twas heaviest sorrow.
The king wondered if his sovereign God
he had angered, breaking ancient law,
and embittered the Lord. His breast within
with black thoughts welled; but warlike Beowulf,
plotted vengeance. He bade them work
all iron into a war-shield wondrous: well he knew
that forest-wood against fire was worthless.
A wooden shield could aid not. Earl-king brave,
he was fated to finish this fleeting life,
his days on earth, and the dragon with him,
though long it had watched over its hoard.
Shame he reckoned it to follow the flyer
with a warrior band; nor alone in battle feared he.
Ventures desperate he had passed a-plenty,
perils of war and conqueror proud since
Hrothgar's hall he had wholly purged.

XXIX Beowulf Seeks the Dragon

Safe through many struggles Beowulf
had passed, till this day was come
that doomed him now with the dragon to strive.
With comrades eleven the lord of Geats
swollen in rage went seeking the dragon.
He had heard whence all the harm arose
and the killing of clansmen; that cup of price
on the lap of his master had been laid by the finder.

In the throng he was, the thirteenth man,
starter of all the strife and ill,
care-laden captive; cringing thence
forced and reluctant, he led them on
till he came in sight of that cavern-hall,
the barrow delved near billowy surges,
flood of ocean. Within 'twas full
of wire-gold and jewels; a jealous warden,
warrior trusty, the treasures held,
lurked in his lair. Not light the task
of entrance for any of earth-born men.

Sat on the headland was Beowulf,
the hero king, and friend of all Geats.
All gloomy his soul, wavering, death-bound,
but he spoke, and a battle-vow made,
his last of all: 'I have lived through many
wars in my youth; now once again,
old folk-defender, feud will I seek,
do brave deeds, if the dark destroyer
forth from his cavern come to fight me!'
Then hailed he the helmeted heroes all,
for the last time greeting his liegemen dear,
comrades of war: 'I should carry no weapon,
no sword to the serpent, if sure I knew
how, with such enemy, else my vows
I could gain as I did in Grendel's day.
But fire in this fight I must fear me now,
and poisonous breath; so I bring with me
breastplate and shield. From the barrow keeper's
flame I will not flee. One fight shall end
our war by the cliff wall. My mood is bold
but forbears to do warn of this battling-flyer.
Now abide by the barrow, ye heroes in harness,
the fight is not yours, nor meet for any but me alone
to measure might with this monster here

and play the hero. Hardily I shall win that wealth,
or war shall seize, cruel killing, your king and lord!'

Up stood then with iron shield the sturdy champion,
and brave under helmet in battle-mail he went,
under steep stone cliffs: no coward's path!
Soon spied by the wall, that warrior chief,
a stream which broke from the barrow.
The brooklet's wave was hot with fire. The hoard
unharmed that way he could never get near.
From deep within his breast, he shouted with rage;
stern it went ringing, his cry loud and clear
beneath the cliff-rocks grey. The hoard-serpent heard
a human voice; his anger was enkindled. No respite now
for pact of peace! The poison-breath
of that foul worm first came forth from the cave,
hot reek-of-fight: the rocks resounded.

Stout by the stone-way his shield he raised,
king of the Geats, against the loathed-one;
while with courage keen that coiled foe
came seeking strife. The sturdy lord
had drawn his sword, not dull of edge,
heirloom old; and each of the two
felt fear of his foe, though fierce their mood.
Stoutly stood with his shield high-raised
the warrior king, as the dragon now coiled
together amain: the mailed-one waited.

Now, scale by scale, fast sped and glided
that blazing serpent. The iron shield protected,
soul and body a shorter while
for the hero-king than his heart desired.
His arm he lifted and struck with his sword.
Its edge was turned, dull blade on bone,
biting more feebly than its noble master needed.

45

Then the barrow's keeper waxed full wild
from that weighty blow, cast deadly flames;
wide drove and far those vicious fires.
No victor's glory the Geats' lord boasted;
his sword had failed, as never it should.

'Twas no easy path Beowulf must tread to face his foe.
Not long it was before they grimly closed again.
The dragon was heartened; high heaved his breast
and enfolded in flames brave Beowulf.
Sorrow the king suffered, encircled with fire
while thanes ran for the woods, their lives to save.
But the soul of one thane with care was encumbered,
for kinship can never waver in he who is proper.

XXX Wiglaf the Trusty

WIGLAF his name was, Weohstan's son,
his king and kinsman he now saw hard oppressed.
He recalled the prizes his lord had given him,
and not long he lingered. His wooden shield he seized;
the old sword he drew. For the first time now
with Beowulf the young thane
was to share the shock of battle.
Wiglaf spoke, and his words were wise:
'I remember the time, when mead we took,
what promise we made to our king
to give him allegiance with sword and shield.
Now the day is come that our noble master
has need of the might of warriors stout.
Let us stride along the hero to help
while the heat is about him glowing and grim.
For God is my witness I would far more rather
the fire should seize along with my lord
these limbs of mine! My sword and helmet,
breastplate and board, for us both shall serve!'

Through slaughter-reek strode he to aid his chieftain,
his battle-helmet on, and brief words spoke:
'Beowulf, do all bravely, and with all thy strength
shield thy life! I will stand to help thee.'

At the words the serpent came once again,
murderous monster mad with rage,
with fire-billows flaming, its foes to seek,
the hated men. In heat-waves burned
Wiglaf's shield and the breastplate failed
to shelter at all the spear-thane young.
Yet quickly under his king's shield
went the eager earl, since his own was now
all burned by the blaze. The bold king again
had mind of his glory: with might his sword
was driven into the dragon's head,
blow nerved by hate. But Naegling shivered,
broken in battle was Beowulf's blade,
old and grey. 'Twas granted him not
that ever the edge of iron at all
could help him at strife: too strong was his hand,
so the tale is told, and he tried too far
with strength of stroke all swords he wielded,
though sturdy their steel. Then for the third time
that folk-destroyer, fire-dread dragon,
rushed on the hero, where room allowed,
battle-grim, burning; its bitter teeth
closed on Beowulf's neck, and his battle-mail
was soon covered with waves of blood.

XXXI The Fatal Struggle

'TWAS now Wiglaf made known his
craft and keenness and courage enduring.
Heedless of harm, though his hand was burned,
hardy-hearted, he smote with sword

47

a little lower the loathsome beast;
his steel drove in bright and burnished;
that blaze began to lose and lessen.
The king wielded his wits again, war-knife drew,
a biting blade by his breastplate hanging,
and smote that serpent asunder,
felled the foe, flung forth its life.
So had they killed it, kinsmen both.
Yet of deeds of valour this conqueror's-hour
was Beowulf's last. The wound
which the dragon-of-earth had inflicted,
began to swell and smart; and soon he found
the blood in his chest was boiling,
pain of poison. The king walked on,
wise in his thought, to the wall of rock;
then sat, and stared at the structure of giants,
where arch of stone and steadfast column
upheld forever that hall in earth.

The king and conqueror covered with blood,
with struggle spent, untied his helmet.
Beowulf spoke in spite of his hurt,
his mortal wound; full well he knew
his portion now was past and gone
of earthly bliss, and all had fled
of his file of days, and death was near:
'My son I would give now this gear of war,
had any heirs been granted me. This people I ruled
fifty winters. Feuds I sought not,
nor falsely swore an oath. From the Ruler-of-Man
no wrath shall seize me, when life from my frame
must flee. Now go, gaze on the hoard under the rock.
And fare, Wiglaf, in haste. I would like to behold
the gorgeous heirlooms, golden store;
have joy in the jewels and gems; lay down
softly for my dying sight the costly treasure.'

XXXII Beowulf's Death

I HAVE heard that swiftly Wiglaf,
at wish and word of his wounded king,
entered the barrow, saw store of jewels
and glistening gold, unburnished bowls of bygone men,
rusty helmets of the olden age; and arm-rings
wondrously woven. His glance fell onto a golden banner
of handiwork noblest, brilliantly embroidered; so bright
its gleam, all the earth-floor he easily saw
and viewed all these vessels. Nothing now
was seen of the serpent: the sword had taken him.
Then he burdened his bosom with beakers and plate,
hasted the herald, the hoard so spurred him,
his track to retrace; he was troubled by doubt,
high-souled hero, if haply he'd find
alive, where he left him, the lord of the Geats.

So he carried the load and his leader and king
he found all bleeding, weakening fast
by the wall of the cave. The liegeman
splashed him with water, till point of word
broke through the breast-hoard. Beowulf spoke,
sage and sad, as he stared at the gold.
'For the gold and treasure, to God my thanks
for what I behold, to Heaven's Lord,
for the grace that I give such gifts to my folk.
Now I've bartered here for booty of treasure
the last of my life, so look ye well
to the needs of my land. No longer I tarry.
A barrow I bid ye raise for my ashes.
'Twill shine by the shore of the sea,
to folk of mine memorial fair
on the whales' headland high uplifted,
that ocean-wanderers often may hail
Beowulf's Barrow, as back from afar

---

they drive their ships over the darkling wave.'
From his neck he unclasped the collar of gold,
valorous king, to Wiglaf gave it
with bright-gold helmet, breastplate, and ring,
to the youthful thane he bade him use them in joy.
'You are the end, the last of my kin,
for fate hath swept all of my line,
to the land of doom and I go after them.'
These words were the last which Beowulf said.
His soul, be it saintly, from his bosom fled.

XXXIII Wiglaf Speaks his Mind

THE young hero gazed at the sorrowful sight,
his lord beloved lying still on the cold earth.
But the slayer too, awful earth-dragon,
empty of breath, lay felled in fight.
For edges of iron had ended its days,
hard and battle-sharp, blades piercing;
and that flier-afar had fallen to ground
hushed by its hurt, its hoard all near,
no longer lusty aloft to whirl
at midnight, making its merriment seen,
proud of its prizes: prone it sank
by the handiwork of the hero-king.

The cowardly thanes came out of the thicket,
ten together, fearing before to flourish a spear
in the sore distress of their sovereign lord.
Now in their shame their shields they carried,
armour of fight, where the old man lay;
and they gazed on Wiglaf. Wearied he sat
at his sovereign's shoulder, shieldsman good,
to revive him with water. Nowise it availed.
Though well he wished it, never could he
change the will of the all-wielding God.

Wiglaf spoke, mournful he looked
on those men unloved: 'The king who gave you
the armour of war in which ye stand,
for he at ale-bench often-times bestowed
on hall-folk helmet and breastplate,
threw away and wasted these spoils of war,
on men who failed when the enemy came!
To rescue his life, 'twas little that I
could serve him in struggle; yet shift I made
(hopeless it seemed) to help my kinsman.
Its strength then waned, when with weapon I struck
that fatal foe, and the fire less strongly
flowed from its head. Too few the heroes
in the midst of battle that thronged to our king!
Now gift of treasure and giving of sword,
joy of the house and home-delight
shall fail your folk; his freehold-land
every clansman within your kin
shall lose and leave, when lords high-born
hear afar of that flight of yours,
a fameless deed. Yea, death is better
for liegemen all than a life of shame!'

XXXIV The Messenger of Death

THAT battle-toil Wiglaf announced,
at the fort on the cliff, where, full of sorrow,
all morning the earls had sat, wondering whether
they would wail as dead, or welcome back,
their lord beloved. Then the herald up the headland rode,
telling all: 'Now the Lord of Geats on the slaughter-bed sleeps
by the serpent's deed! And beside him is stretched
that slayer-of-men with knife-wounds sick.
There Wiglaf sitteth by Beowulf's side,
the living earl by the other dead and, heavy of heart,
a death-watch keeps over friend and foe.'

XXXV The Funeral Pyre

Now haste is best, for a season of strife is expected,
and we go to gaze on our Geatish lord,
and bear the bountiful giver of rings
to the funeral pyre. No fragments merely
shall burn with the warrior. Wealth of jewels,
gold untold and gained in terror,
treasure at last with his life obtained,
all of that booty the brands shall take,
fire shall eat it. No earl must carry
memorial jewel. No maiden fair
shall wreathe her neck with noble ring:
nay, sad in spirit and shorn of her gold,
often shall she pass over paths of exile
lamenting her loss of lord and laughter.
Hence many a war-spear, cold from the morning,
shall be clutched in the fingers of foes.

Wiglaf spoke: 'This hoard is ours
but grievously gotten; too grim the fate
which thither carried our king and lord.
I was within there, and all I viewed,
the chambered treasure, when chance allowed me
under the earth-wall. Eager, I seized
such heap from the hoard as hands could bear
and hurriedly carried it hither back
to my liege and lord. Alive was he still,
still wielding his wits. The wise old man
spoke much in his sorrow, and sent you greetings
and bade that ye build, when he breathed no more,
at the place near his death a barrow high,
memorial mighty. Of men was he
worthiest warrior wide earth over.
Let us set out in haste now, the second time
to see and search this store of treasure,

those wall-hid wonders, the way I show you,
where, ye may gaze your fill at golden rings.'

But few found joy in the hollowed caverns
and the dragon they cast, the foul worm,
over the wall for the waves to take,
and they all watched the green surges swallow
that shepherd of spellbound gems.

XXXVI The Burning of Beowulf

THEN fashioned for Beowulf, the folk of Geats,
firm on the earth, a funeral-pile,
and hung it with helmets and harness of war
and breastplates bright, as the boon he asked;
and they laid amid it the mighty chieftain,
heroes mourning their master dear.
Then wood-smoke rose black over blaze,
and blended was the roar of flame with weeping
till the fire had broken the frame of bones,
hot at the heart. In a heavy mood they moaned
their misery. Wailing her woe, the widow old,
her hair upbound, for Beowulf's death
sung in her sorrow, and said full oft
she dreaded the doleful days to come.
The smoke by the sky was devoured.
The folk of the Geats fashioned there
on the headland a barrow broad and high,
by ocean-farers far could see.
In ten days' time their toil had raised it,
the battle-brave's beacon. Round the pyre
a wall they built, the worthiest ever
that wit could prompt in their wisest men.
They placed in the barrow that precious booty,
the treasure from the hoard in the cave,
trusting the ground with the wealth of earls,

gold in the earth, where ever it lies
useless to men as of yore it was.
Then about that barrow the battle-keen rode,
a band of twelve, lamenting and mourning their king,
chanting their dirge, and the honour spent.
Thus made their mourning for their hero's passing,
Beowulf, the bravest and most beloved of men.

End Notes

When Beowulf returns to Sweden he gives his uncle, King Hygelac, not mere gossip of his journey, but a statesman-like forecast of the outcome of certain policies at the Danish court.

After Beowulf is made king we have the old myth of a dragon who guards hidden treasure (a myth touched upon in XIII). But with this runs the story of an earl, last of his race, who hides all his wealth within this barrow and there chants his farewell to life's glories. After his death the dragon takes possession of the hoard and watches over it. A condemned or banished man, desperate, hides in the barrow, discovers the treasure, and while the dragon sleeps, makes off with a golden beaker and carries it to his master in the hope of placating him. The dragon discovers the loss and exacts a fearful penalty from the people round about.

Some critics have been keen to point out the strongly heathen character of the end of the epic. Beowulf's death came, so the old tradition ran, from his unwitting interference with spell-bound treasure. And it is only after Beowulf's death do we have a clear reference to his wife. Critics tend to agree that Beowulf accepted Hygd's offer of the kingdom after her son's death and, as was customary, he married her.

Brief Summary

Beowulf voyages to Heorot, Hrothgar's hall. There he destroys Grendel, who for twelve years has haunted the hall by night and slain all he found therein. When Grendel's mother in revenge makes an attack on the hall, Beowulf seeks her out and kills her also in her home beneath the waters. He then returns to his land with honour and is rewarded by his king Hygelac. Ultimately he himself becomes king of the Geats, and fifty years later slays a dragon and is slain by it. The poem closes with an account of the funeral rites.

Glossary of Names

Aeschere: confidential friend of Hrothgar. Killed by Grendel.

Beow: Son of Scyld, the founder of the dynasty of Scyldings. Grandfather of Hrothgar.

Beowulf: The hero of the poem is sprung from the stock of Geats. He is the son of Ecgtheow, but is brought up by his maternal grandfather Hrethel. A hero from his youth, he has the strength of thirty men. He engages in a swimming-match with Breca and goes to the help of Hrothgar against the monster Grendel. Several references are made to Beowulf's helmet which has several boar-images on it (the boar was sacred to Freyr, who was the favourite god of the Germanic tribes about the North Sea and the Baltic). He vanquishes Grendel and his mother and afterwards becomes king of the Geats. Late in life he attempts to kill a fire-spewing dragon, and is slain. Beowulf is buried with great honours.

Breca: Beowulf's opponent in the famous swimming-match.

Cain: progenitor of Grendel and other monsters. Son of Adam.

Danes: subjects of Scyld and his descendants, and hence often called Scyldings.

Ecglaf: father of Unferth.

Ecgtheow: father of Beowulf, the hero of the poem. After slaying Heatholaf, a Wylfing, he flees his country.

Geats: the Swedish race to which the hero of the poem belongs. Also called Weder-Geats, or Sea-Geats. They are ruled by Hygelac and then Beowulf.

Grendel: monster of the race of Cain. Dwells in the fens and moors. Is furiously envious when he hears sounds of joy in Hrothgar's palace. Causes the king untold agony for years. Is finally conquered by Beowulf, and dies of his wound. His hand and arm are hung up in Hrothgar's hall Heorot. His head is cut off by Beowulf when he goes down to fight with Grendel's mother.

Helmings: the race to which Queen Wealhtheow belonged.

Healfdene: grandson of Scyld and father of Hrothgar. Ruled the Danes long and well.

Heorot: the great mead-hall which King Hrothgar builds. It is invaded by Grendel for twelve years. Finally cleansed by Beowulf, the Geat. It is called Heorot on account of the hart-antlers which decorate it. The building would have been rectangular, with opposite doors - west and east - and a hearth in the middle of the single room. A row of pillars down each side, at some distance from the walls, made a space which was raised a little above the main floor, and was furnished with two rows of seats. On one side, usually south, was the high-seat midway between the doors. Opposite this, on the other raised space, was another seat of honour. At the banquet described Hrothgar would have sat in the south or chief high-seat, with Beowulf opposite to him. Planks on trestles formed the tables just in front of the long rows of seats, and were taken away after banquets, when the retainers were ready to stretch themselves out for sleep on the benches.

Hrethel: King of the Geats, father of Hygelac, and grandfather of Beowulf.

Hrothgar: the Danish king who built the hall Heorot, but was unable to enjoy it on account of Grendel. Marries Wealhtheow, a Helming lady. He has two sons and a daughter and is a typical Teutonic king, lavish of gifts.

Hrothmund: son of Hrothgar.

Hrunting: Unferth's sword, lent to Beowulf.

Hygelac: King of the Geats, uncle and liegelord of Beowulf, the hero of the poem. His second wife is the lovely Hygd. Their son of their union is slain in a war with the Franks and Frisians. Beowulf is afterwards king of the Geats.

Hygd: wife of Hygelac. There are some indications that she married Beowulf after she became a widow.

Nægling: Beowulf's sword.

Scyld: founder of the dynasty to which Hrothgar, his father, and grandfather belonged. He dies, and his body is put on a vessel, and set adrift. He goes from Daneland just as he had come to it, in a bark (boat).

Scyldings: the descendants of Scyld. In the poem they are also called Honour-Scyldings, Victory-Scyldings, War-Scyldings, etc.

Unferth: son of Ecglaf, and seemingly a confidential courtier of Hrothgar. Taunts Beowulf for having taken part in the swimming-match. Lends Beowulf his sword when he goes to look for Grendel's mother.

Wealhtheow: wife of Hrothgar. Her queenly courtesy is well shown in the poem.

Wiglaf: son of Wihstan, and related to Beowulf. He remains faithful to Beowulf in the fatal struggle with the fire-drake. Would rather die than leave his lord in his dire emergency.

List of Words and Phrases not in General Use

Atheling: prince, nobleman.
Bairn: son, child.
Bark: ship.
Barrow: mound, rounded hill, funeral-mound.
Beaker: cup, drinking-vessel.
Board: shield.
Bone-house: a kenning for the body.
Earl: nobleman, any brave man.
Hilt: handle of a sword. Sometimes used to represent a sword.
Liegeman: loyal warrior.
Mead: an alcoholic drink made by fermenting honey with water.
Mere: sea; in compounds, 'mere-ways,' 'mere-maid,' etc.
Sail-road: sea.
Thane: thanes swore loyalty to their king or lord, for whom they fought and whom they protected. In return the king was expected to be generous with gifts of treasure and land. The king also protected his thanes. Kings were highly praised for their generosity and hospitality. Warriors were expected to be brave, courageous, and loyal.
Whale-road: ocean or sea, from the Anglo-Saxon *hron-rade*. This is one of the best known kennings in *Beowulf*.
Word-hoard: a kenning for vocabulary

Kennings

Kennings figure heavily in *Beowulf*. They are evocative poetic descriptions of everyday things, often created to fill the alliterative requirements of the metre. For example, a poet might call the sea the 'swan-road' or the 'whale-road'; a king might be called a 'ring-giver.' The device is typically found in many Old English or Anglo-Saxon poems.

Outline of the Story

Hrothgar, king of the Danes, or Scyldings, builds a great mead-hall, or palace, in which he hopes to feast his liegemen and to give them presents. The joy of king and retainers is, however, of short duration. Grendel, the monster, is seized with hateful jealousy. He cannot abide the sounds of the celebration which reach him down in his fen-dwelling near the hall. In anger Grendel goes to the joyous building, bent on direful mischief. Thane after thane is ruthlessly carried off and devoured, while no one is found strong enough and bold enough to cope with the monster. For twelve years he persecutes Hrothgar and the Scyldings.

Over sea, a day's voyage off, Beowulf, nephew of Hygelac, king of the Geats, hears of Grendel's doings and of Hrothgar's misery. He resolves to crush the foul monster and relieve the aged king. With fourteen chosen companions, he sets sail for Dane-land. Reaching that country, he soon persuades Hrothgar of his ability to help him. When Hrothgar departs he leaves the hall in charge of Beowulf, telling him that never before has he given to another the absolute wardship of his palace. All retire to rest, Beowulf, as it were, sleeping upon his arms.

Grendel comes, the great march-stepper, and kills one of the sleeping warriors. Then he advances towards Beowulf. A fierce and desperate hand-to-hand struggle ensues. No arms are used, both combatants trusting to strength and handgrip. Beowulf tears Grendel's shoulder from its socket, and the monster retreats to his den, howling and yelling with agony and fury. The wound is fatal.

The next morning, at early dawn, warriors in numbers flock to the hall Heorot, to hear the news. Joy is boundless. Glee runs high. Hrothgar and his retainers are lavish of gratitude and of gifts.

Grendel's mother, however, comes the next night to avenge his death. She is furious and raging. While Beowulf is sleeping in a room somewhat apart from the quarters of the other warriors, she seizes one of Hrothgar's favourite counsellors, and carries him off and devours him. Beowulf is called. Determined to leave Heorot entirely purified, he arms himself, and goes down to look for the female monster. After traveling through the waters many hours, he meets her near the sea-bottom. She drags him to her den. There he sees Grendel lying dead. After a desperate and almost fatal struggle with the woman, he slays her, and swims upward in triumph, taking with him Grendel's head.

Joy is renewed at Heorot. Congratulations crowd upon the victor. Hrothgar literally pours treasures into the lap of Beowulf; and it is agreed among the vassals of the king that Beowulf will be their next liegelord. Beowulf leaves Daneland and Hrothgar weeps and laments at his departure.

When the hero arrives in his own land, Hygelac treats him as a distinguished guest. He is the hero of the hour.

Beowulf subsequently becomes king of his own people, the Geats. After he has been ruling for fifty years, a fire-spewing dragon woefully harries his own neighbourhood. Beowulf determines to kill him. In the ensuing struggle both Beowulf and the dragon are slain. The grief of the Geats is inexpressible. They determine, however, to leave nothing undone to honour the memory of their lord. A great funeral-pyre is built, and his body is burnt. Then a memorial-barrow is made, visible from a great distance, that sailors afar may be constantly reminded of the prowess of the national hero of Geatland.

The poem closes with a glowing tribute to his bravery, his gentleness, his goodness of heart, and his generosity.

The History of Beowulf

Beowulf is an Old English or Anglo-Saxon* epic poem consisting of just over 3,000 lines. It is the oldest surviving long poem in Old English and is commonly cited as one of the most important works of Old English literature. It was written in England some time between the 8th and the early 11th century.

The events in the poem take place in the late 5th century, after the Anglo-Saxons had started their journey to England, and before the beginning of the 7th century, a time when the Anglo-Saxon people were either newly arrived or still in close contact with their Germanic kinsmen in Northern Germany. The poem may have been brought to England by people of Geatish origins. It has been suggested that *Beowulf* was first composed in the 7th century at Rendlesham in East Anglia, as the Sutton Hoo ship-burial also shows close connections with Scandinavia.

The poem deals with legends, was composed for entertainment, and does not separate between fictional elements and real historic events, for example many of the characters in *Beowulf* also appear in Scandinavian sources. Recently the dating of the events in the poem has been confirmed by archaeological excavations of barrows and in Denmark excavations at Lejre, where Scandinavian tradition located the seat of the Scyldings, i.e., Heorot, have revealed that a hall was built in the mid-6th century, exactly the time period of *Beowulf.*

* Anglo-Saxon, as Cambridge calls it, or Old English, as Oxford prefers to label it.

The Writing of Beowulf

The *Beowulf* manuscript was transcribed from an original by two Anglo-Saxon Christian scribes, one of whom wrote the first two-thirds of the poem and a second who wrote the remainder, with a difference in handwriting noticeable after line 1939. While both scribes appear to have proofread their work, there are nevertheless a number of errors. The work of the second scribe bears a striking resemblance to the work of the first scribe of the Blickling homilies, and so much so that it is believed they derive from the same scriptorium. From knowledge of books held in the library at Malmesbury Abbey and available as source works, and from the identification of certain words particular to the local dialect found in the text, the transcription may have been made there. However, for at least a century, some scholars have maintained that the description of Grendel's lake in Beowulf was borrowed from St. Paul's vision of Hell in Homily 16 of the Blickling homilies.

As the critic Terry Eagleton noted: *Beowulf* accommodates conflicting realities, pagan and Christian, within a single order. It is written by a Christian poet about the pre-Christian past of his people, and thus combines historical detachment and imaginative inwardness.

The full poem survives in the manuscript known as the Nowell Codex, located in the British Library. It has no title in the original manuscript, but has become known by the name of the story's protagonist. In 1731, the manuscript was badly damaged by a fire that swept through Ashburnham House in London that had a collection of medieval manuscripts assembled by Sir Robert Bruce Cotton.

The Beowulf Legend

The word legend has a very interesting history, which sheds light not only on its origin but on early habits of thought and customs. It is derived from the Latin verb *legere*, which means 'to read.' As legends are often passed down by word of mouth and are not reduced to writing until they have been known for centuries by great numbers of people, it seems difficult at first glance to see any connection between the Latin word and its English descendant.

The legend is not so sharply defined as the myth and the fairy story, and it is not always possible to separate it from these old forms of stories; but it always concerns itself with one or more characters; it assumes to be historical; it is almost always old and haunts some locality like a ghost; and it has a large mixture of fiction. Like the myth and fairy story it throws light on the mind and character of the age that produced it; it is part of the history of the unfolding of the human mind in the world; and, above all, it is fascinating.

Fascinating as *Beowulf* is the narrative plays out against a background of what appears to be fact. Incidentally, and in a number of digressions (few of which are included within the abridged version), we receive much information about the Geats and Danes: all of which information has an appearance of historic accuracy, and in some cases can be proved, from external evidence, to be historically accurate. For example, Hygelac's capital was probably not far from the modern Göteborg and several of the kings mentioned in the poem, such as the English King Offa, are well documented. But in none of the accounts of Scandinavian kings, whether written in Norse or monkish Latin, is there mention of any name corresponding to that of Beowulf, as king of the Geats.

However, it has been generally held that the Beowulf of the poem is compounded out of two elements: that an historic Beowulf, king of the Geats, has been combined with a mythological figure Beowa, a god of the ancient Angles; that the historical achievements against Frisians and Swedes belong to the king, the mythological adventures with giants and dragons to the god.

Yet what tells against Beowulf as a historic Geatic king is that there is always apt to be something extravagant and unreal about what the poem tells us of his deeds, contrasting with the sober and historic way in which other kings, like Hrothgar or Hygelac, are referred to. But we must not disqualify Beowulf simply because he slew a dragon; so sober an authority as the *Anglo-Saxon Chronicle* assures us that fiery dragons were flying in Northumbria as late as 793.

Studying Beowulf

Writing in 1887 of the proposal to establish an Anglo-Saxon-based school of English at Oxford, one professor protested that 'an English School will grow up, nourishing our language not from the humanity of the Greeks and Romans, but from the savagery of the Goths and Anglo-Saxons. We are about to reverse the Renaissance.' With its Teutonic barbarians and earthy, violent behaviour there was the fear of moral corruption coming from the study of Anglo-Saxon literature. Yet from *Beowulf*, and canny, virile stories like it, have emerged wonderful novels from the Anglo-Saxonist J.R.R. Tolkien and the medievalist C.S. Lewis.

Notable Cinema, Television and Novel Adaptations

Beowulf (1999): a science-fiction/fantasy film starring Christopher Lambert.

Beowulf (2007): an American 3D motion capture epic fantasy film directed by Robert Zemeckis and written by Neil Gaiman and Roger Avary.

Beowulf (2013): a novel adaptation by Michael Murpurgo.

Beowulf (2016 TV series): an ITV adaptation currently in post-production - starring Kieran Bew as Beowulf.

The 2007 animated *Beowulf*, starring Ray Winstone as the eponymous character and Anthony Hopkins as Hrothgar, is probably the most well known adaptation. However, it does differ significantly from the original poem. Neil Gaiman and Roger Avary have justified these choices by arguing that Beowulf acts as an unreliable narrator in the portion of the poem in which he describes his battle with Grendel's mother. Some of the changes made in the film include:

the portrayal of Hrothgar as a womanizing alcoholic
the portrayal of Unferth as a Christian
the early appearance of Wiglaf
the portrayal of Grendel's mother as a beautiful seductress who bears Grendel as Hrothgar's child and the dragon as Beowulf's child
Beowulf's funeral

Anglo-Saxon Riddles

To the Anglo-Saxons the wisdom of a people, with their stories, riddles and songs, was carried mentally, orally, in the word-hoard or treasure-house of words, the individual and collective memory of the tribe. This word-hoard was invisible but priceless, and also invincible. You couldn't see it, you couldn't steal it, you couldn't kill it; you could only hear it, remember it, cherish it, and pass it down from generation to generation. Below are seven riddles, some easier than others. The answers are given on page 80, but if you find them too challenging there are clues in the next paragraph.

With the first riddle you should be able to work out the ingredient that is taken from the woods. It is then made into something which is enjoyed in Heorot. The second riddle is about a creature which the monks, with their books, would have been all too familiar with. The third riddle needs careful consideration. It is both a destroyer and a friend. D should be very easy. E is often found in the kitchen. The penultimate riddle (F) is about something mentioned several times in Beowulf. The last one (G) is a type of bird.

A

I am man's treasure, taken from the woods,
cliff-sides, hill-slopes, valleys, downs;
by day wings bear me in the buzzing air,
slip me under a sheltering roof - sweet craft.
Soon a man bears me to a tub. Bathed,
I am binder and scourge of men, bring down
the young, ravage the old, sap strength.
Soon he discovers who wrestles with me
my fierce body-rush - I roll fools
flush on the ground. Robbed of strength,
reckless of speech, a man knows no power
Over hands, feet, mind. Who am I who bind

men on middle-earth, blinding with rage
and such savage blows that dazed
fools know my dark power by daylight?

B

A moth ate songs - wolfed words!
That seemed a weird dish - that a worm
should swallow, dumb thief in the dark,
the songs of a man, his chants of glory,
their place of strength. That thief-guest
was no wiser for having swallowed words.

C

A wonderful warrior exists on earth.
Two dumb creatures make him grow bright between them.
Enemies use him against one another.
His strength is fierce but a woman can tame him.
He will meekly serve both men and women
If they know the trick of looking after him
And feeding him properly.
He makes people happy.
He makes their lives better.
But if they let him grow proud
This ungrateful friend soon turns against them.

D

Four dilly-dandies (teats on the udder)
Four stick standies (legs)
Two crookers (horns)
Two lookers (eyes)
And a wig wag (tail)

E

When I am alive I do not speak.
Anyone who wants to takes me captive and cuts off my head.
They bite my bare body
I do no harm to anyone unless they cut me first.
Then I soon make them cry.

F

I am all on my own.
Wounded by iron weapons and scarred by swords.
I often see battle. I am tired of fighting.
I do not expect to be allowed to retire from warfare
Before I am completely done for.
At the wall of the city, I am knocked about
And bitten again and again.
Hard edged things made by the blacksmith's hammer attack
me. Each time I wait for something worse.
I have never been able to find a doctor who could make me
better, or give me medicine made from herbs.
Instead the sword gashes all over me grow bigger day and
night.

G

I was abandoned by my mother and father.
I wasn't yet breathing. A kind woman
Covered me with clothes, kept me and looked after me,
Cuddled me as close as if I had been her own child.
Under that covering I grew and grew.
I was unkind to my adopted brothers and sisters.
This lovely woman fed me
Until I was big enough to set out on my own.
She had fewer of her own dear sons and daughters because she
did so.

The Anglo-Saxon Language

Anglo-Saxon is gnarled, racy, muscular and robust. Unlike cerebral, anaemic languages such as French, Anglo-Saxon words in *Beowulf* sound, according to one critic, rather like the rumbling of a sack of potatoes being emptied. Words tend to be short, just one or two syllables (mono or disyllabic). They include words about the body, farming, the weather, relations and the landscape. Below are some examples:

A   abide, above, ale
B   back, bath, bed
C   can, carve, cobweb
D   daft, daughter, dead
E   each, ear, elbow
F   fair, fall, feather
G   game, gate, god
H   hammer, harbour, hand, hate
I   I, it, if,
K   keen, keep, kind
L   ladle, land, laugh, love
M   make, man, marsh
N   nail, name, needle
O   oak, of, on
P   path, pin, pipe
Q   queen, quick
R   rag, rain, rat
S   say, see, send
T   take, thank, thimble
U   udder, under, up
V   vat
W   woman, wake, walk
Y   yard, yes, yawn

Anglo-Saxon words now only make up about 30% of our vocabulary, yet it is hard to make up a sentence without them.

Essay Questions and Creative Tasks

What are the qualities in the character of Beowulf that we are encouraged to admire?

Consider the female characters in *Beowulf*, including Grendel's mother. What do they contribute to the narrative?

Consider the significance of bravery within *Beowulf*. Comment on the eponymous character, Wiglaf as a young warrior, and the cowardly thanes at the end of the poem.

How significant is the setting within *Beowulf*?

How does the poem explore the theme of revenge? Consider Grendel, Grendel's mother, the dragon and Beowulf.

Imagine you have been asked to produce a film adaptation of *Beowulf*. What changes would you make to the poem?

Imagine you are a film producer about to cast *Beowulf*. Write a letter to an actor or actress asking them to play a particular part in your forthcoming adaptation. Explain why you have chosen them, where you'll be shooting your film and which themes you hope to explore.

Interview Beowulf after he has defeated Grendel in the mead-hall. Write out the script and include other characters in your TV or radio interview.

Research Topics

Anglo-Saxon Words
Months of the Year
Days of the Week

Woodcut depicting Odin followed by a berserker. Beserkers were Vikings who, according to numerous Old Norse sources, fought in a trance-like fury. The modern word berserk (to go beserk) comes from the Norse, though the original word meant a bear or bare-coated (bare-chested) warrior.

Answers to the Riddles

A   This powerful creature is mead made from honey, a favourite Anglo-Saxon drink. There is evidence of Germanic tribes keeping bees for honey as far back as the fourth century B.C. The number of mead compounds in Old English attests to its central place in the culture. Comrades come to the mead-hall on the mead-path, sit at mead-benches, drinking from mead-cups and getting head-high until they drop, mead-weary.

B   This is a riddle from the 1,000 year-old Exeter Book manuscript in Exeter Cathedral in Devonshire. The thief who swallows songs is a bookworm. The riddler pokes fun at the pedantic worm, transformed into word-wolf or midnight marauder, who devours the substance without the spirit.

The medieval moth lays its eggs in a manuscript whose vellum pages are made of cowhide. There are many riddles about books and bookmaking in the Middle Ages. What enclosed the cow, its skin, becomes a path of learning, the page, over which the tailfeather of a bird, the quill, tracks juice from the bark of the hawthorne, the ink. This produces knowledge none of which the bookworm cares about. The moth larvae hatch and eat the pages, devouring the text without understanding.

This riddle may be derived from the 4th or 5th century Latin riddle of Symphosius which reads in translation:

Writing has nourished me, yet I know no letters.
I've lived in books, yet I've learned nothing.
I've devoured the muses, yet I'm unenlightened.

C   Fire
D   A cow or a goat.
E   An onion
F   A shield
G   A cuckoo

Bibliography

Damico, Helen (1984), *Beowulf's Wealhtheow and the Valkyrie Tradition*, University of Wisconsin Press.

Nicholson, Lewis E, ed. (1963), *An Anthology of Beowulf Criticism*, University of Notre Dame Press.

North, Richard (2006), *The King's Soul: Danish Mythology in Beowulf, Origins of Beowulf: From Vergil to Wiglaf*, Oxford University Press.

Orchard, Andy (2003), *A Critical Companion to Beowulf*, Cambridge.

Tolkien, John Ronald Reuel (1958). *Beowulf: The Monsters and the Critics and other essays*, Harper Collins.

My special thanks are due to Stephen Bywater for his work on the abridged version. I must also thank Francis March, James Harrison and Lleslie Hall for their generous assistance. The translation owes much to the work of the late Francis Gummere, professor of English at Haverford College.

Tony Chatterton was born in Nuneaton in 1964. He attended Bosworth College, the University of North London, Leeds University and St Andrews. He now lives with his wife and two daughters in New Bedford, Massachusetts.

Stephen Bywater, with whom he collaborated on this abridged version, is the author of *The Devil's Ark* and *Night of the Damned*.

Made in United States
Orlando, FL
26 April 2022